HAUNTED HOUSES!

SANDRA DOOLING

PowerKiDS
press

New York

Published in 2014 by The Rosen Publishing Group, Inc.
29 East 21st Street, New York, NY 10010

First Edition

Editor: Joanne Randolph
Book Design: Contentra Technologies
Illustrations: Contentra Technologies

Publisher Cataloging Data

Dooling, Sandra.
Haunted houses! / by Sandra Dooling.
p. cm. — (Jr. graphic monster stories)
Includes index.
ISBN 978-1-4777-6199-1 (library binding) — ISBN 978-1-4777-6200-4 (pbk.) —
ISBN 978-1-4777-6201-1 (6-pack)
1. Haunted houses — Juvenile literature. I. Dooling, Sandra. II. Title.
BF1475.D66 2014
133.1 —d23

Manufactured in the United States of America
CPSIA Compliance Information: Batch #W14PK1: For Further Information contact Rosen Publishing,
New York, New York at 1-800-237-9932

Contents

Main Characters

Evelyn Byrd (1707–1737) Died of a broken heart because she was not allowed to marry the man she loved. Her ghost haunts the gardens of Westover Plantation.

William Byrd II (1674–1744) Builder of Westover Plantation and father of Evelyn Byrd and William Byrd III. He refused to allow his daughter Evelyn to marry the man she loved.

William Byrd III (1728–1777) Younger brother of Evelyn Byrd who took his own life at Westover Plantation. His ghost has been seen in the room where he died.

Elizabeth Carter Byrd (1731–1760) First wife of William Byrd III. Killed in a terrible accident, her death cries are still heard at Westover Plantation.

Maria Taylor Byrd (1698–1771) Second wife of William Byrd II and mother of William Byrd III. Her ghost revisits the room where her daughter-in-law, Elizabeth Carter Byrd, died at Westover Plantation.

Anne Carter Harrison (1704–1745) Close friend of Evelyn Byrd who first saw Evelyn's ghost in the gardens of Westover Plantation.

Haunted Houses!

WESTOVER PLANTATION IS LOCATED ON THE JAMES RIVER ABOUT 35 MILES (56 KM) SOUTHEAST OF RICHMOND, VIRGINIA. IT IS A POPULAR VACATION **DESTINATION**.

SO WE ARE FINALLY AT WESTOVER PLANTATION.

THEY SAY IT IS A HAUNTED HOUSE!

HAUNTED **HOAX**, MORE LIKELY.

I'D LIKE TO KNOW MORE ABOUT THIS BEAUTIFUL PLACE.

I CAN HELP YOU.

ISN'T THERE A SAD STORY ABOUT A WOMAN WHO LIVED HERE?

THAT WOULD BE EVELYN BYRD.

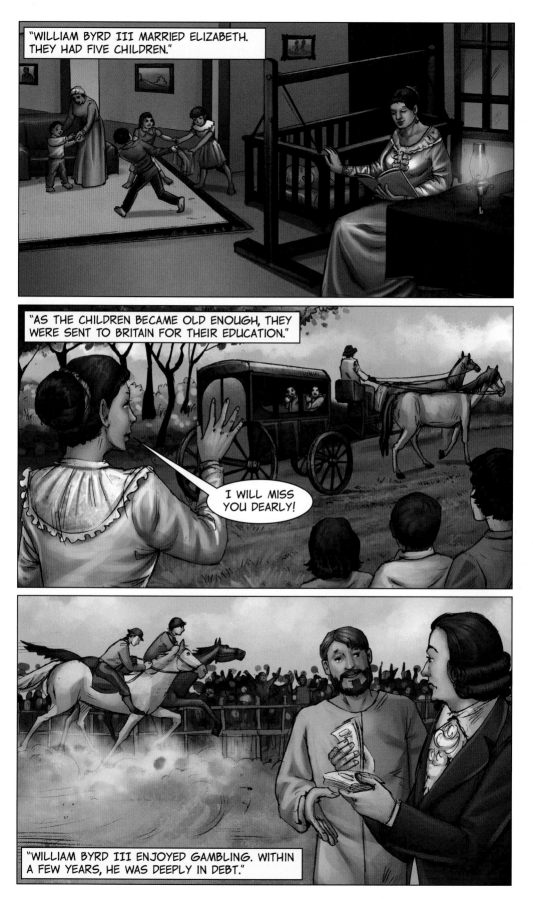

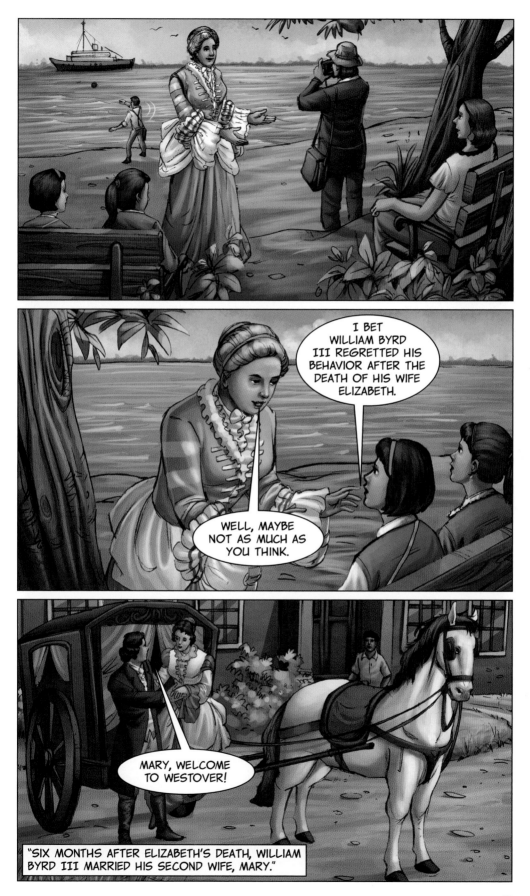

"WILLIAM BYRD III CONTINUED TO GAMBLE AND LOSE MONEY."

"TO PAY HIS DEBTS, WILLIAM BYRD III WAS FORCED TO SELL MUCH OF HIS LAND."

"WILLIAM BYRD III FINALLY BECAME OVERWHELMED BY HIS PROBLEMS."

I OWE EVERYONE MONEY! THERE IS NO WAY OUT FOR ME.

More on Haunted Houses

- People who have experienced haunted houses tell of seeing ghostly figures, hearing strange sounds such as rattling chains, smelling special odors, and feeling sudden chills in the air and even ghostly touches.

- **The Winchester Mystery House**
  One of the most unique haunted houses in the United States is the Winchester Mystery House, in San Jose, California. The house has twisting hallways, secret passageways, and a **séance** room. According to legend, the house was designed to confuse the spirits. During her nightly séance, Mrs. Winchester would receive new building plans from the good spirits. The house is now open for tours. Employees report that locked doors unlock themselves mysteriously, lights come on in the empty house, and a hot meal, such as chicken soup, can be smelled near the empty kitchen.

- **Amityville**
  In November 1974, a young man shot his parents, brothers, and sisters in their home in Amityville, New York. The man claimed that voices had told him to kill his family. The next family to live in the house soon began to hear mysterious voices and see frightening spirits. They experienced **transformations**, **levitations**, a **plague** of flies in winter, loud voices, music, footsteps, and other terrors. **Mediums** became ill after holding séances in the house. Later owners of the house reported no strange experiences, leading many people to wonder if the stories were a hoax.

- **Carson House**
  The Carson House, a three-story mansion in North Carolina, is another famous haunted house. People walking by the house have seen the ghostly figure of a woman dressed in white standing on the front porch. It is thought that she might be the wife of Colonel John Carson, the home's builder. Since she died shortly after her home was built, her ghost may have wanted more time to live there. Some speculate that the lady in white is the ghost of Mary Presnell Carson, mistress of the home when Union soldiers looted it during the Civil War. It is thought that other spirits also walk the plantation.

Glossary

confided (kun-FYD-ed) Told someone secrets or private thoughts.

confined (kun-FYND) Kept in a place.

destination (des-tih-NAY-shun) A place to which a person travels.

hoax (HOHKS) Something that has been faked.

hospitality (hos-pih-TA-luh-tee) The friendly treatment of guests.

inherited (in-HER-it-ed) Received something from a parent.

inseparable (in-SEH-puh-ruh-bul) United and difficult to separate.

levitations (leh-vuh-TAY-shunz) Instances of rising and floating in the air.

meddle (MEH-del) To interest oneself in what is not one's concern.

mediums (MEE-dee-umz) People who thought they could communicate with spirits.

plague (PLAYG) A very bad illness, curse, or hardship.

séance (SAY-ahnts) A meeting in which people try to call up spirits.

transformations (trants-fer-MAY-shunz) Major changes.

ventured (VEN-churd) Undertook something that involves risk or danger.

Index

Websites

Due to the changing nature of Internet links, PowerKids Press has developed an online list of websites related to the subject of this book. This site is updated regularly. Please use this link to access the list:

www.powerkidslinks.com/mons/haunt